To Mar
and Fa

CW01459629

~~~~ ~ ~~ love

Marie | Popsy
x .

Positive Poems

MARIE BYRNE

authorHOUSE®

AuthorHouse™ UK
1663 Liberty Drive
Bloomington, IN 47403 USA
www.authorhouse.co.uk
Phone: UK TFN: 0800 0148641 (Toll Free inside the UK)
        UK Local: 02036 956322 (+44 20 3695 6322 from outside the UK)

Published by AuthorHouse 08/31/2021

ISBN: 978-1-6655-8504-0 (sc)
ISBN: 978-1-6655-8503-3 (e)

Print information available on the last page.

CONTENTS

Love

Variety is the spice of life

Short and Sweet

To Finish

INTRODUCTION

I have written in happy times and also to encourage myself in difficult times.

RAY OF SUNSHINE

Here are a few poems written to make me happy.

JOYS OF LIFE

Waking up to the morning sun
And watching the sun rise,
Seeing that someone loves you
When you look into their eyes,
Hearing my baby's laughter
Is like music to my ears,
And laughing so much
That my eyes well up with tears,
Going to the park and feeding the ducks
Going home and stroking the cat,
Meeting up with your best bud
And having a good chat,
Spending time with the people you love
Knowing God's there
Up above.
Waking up to music
Puts me in a good mood,
And so does eating
My favourite food,
Dancing like you do not care,
When your makeup looks good
And so does your hair,
When someone says the sweetest thing,

When at the top of your voice you do sing,
Walking barefoot on soft sand,
When you need it most someone lending a hand,
When you thought they were lost
Finding your keys,
Teaching your children,
That honey comes from bees,
Flowers, friendships and times that we share,
Knowing that others care,
Soaking in the bath,
Going to sleep with your other half.

LITTLE BIRD

Why do you sing little bird in a tree?
Is it because you are happy to be?
Is it because you have something to say?
Is it because you are cheerful and gay?
Is it to attract a mate?
Are you looking for a hot date?
Are you happy because of the morning sun?
Are you happy because a new days begun?
Are you happy you can feel the breeze?
Are you happy because you live in the trees?
Are you happy because you can fly?
Are you happy because you can soar in the sky?
Are you happy you can sing?
With your friends all day long?
Are you happy because?
You can sing a song?
Are you singing for territory to protect your spot?
Are you looking for a mate?
Saying look at me - I'm hot?
Whatever it is, it makes me smile,
As I listen for a while,
And as I listen,
My heart is filled with good cheer,

Oh, how wonderful it is to hear,
So, why do you sing little bird in a tree?
Perhaps, it will remain a mystery,
You sound like you're singing your heart out with glee,
That's what you sound like to me.

THANK YOU LORD

I, thank you for the animals,
And the fishes in the sea,
I, thank you for making them
And for making me,
I, thank you for my friends and family
Who support me all around,
Cos' not everyone has this
I have found,
I, thank you I have food
For every day of the year,
I, thank you that I will not starve
As others do fear,
I, thank you that you're there for me
Whenever I need you,
I, thank you that you love me
And you love others too,
I, thank you for my home
To protect me from cold and heat,
I, thank you for my clothes and shoes
To protect my body and feet,
I, thank you for pleasures in life
Such as, food and drink; sun and snow,
I, thank you for your blessings,

That others may never know,
I, thank you for the love between:
A husband and his wife,
I, thank you that this brings
Extra joy into our life,
I, thank you for children
They're so innocent and sweet,
I, thank you for my child
Who's loveable and petite,
I, thank you I have two arms and legs
And I can touch, hear and see,
But most of all, I, thank you Lord
Because you died for me.

LITTLE THINGS
MEAN A LOT

A text,
A call,
Standing tall,
Not being late for school,
To breathe,
To rest,
Being prepared
For a test,
To run,
To dance,
A trip,
To France,
To hold a hand,
Walk on the sand,
To paddle or swim,
To go to the gym,
To walk,
To move,
Something improve,
To talk
To laugh
The neck of a giraffe,

The design of creatures
Great and small,
To be outside
And play football,
To drink
To eat,
To walk bare feet,
To listen
To learn,
The smell of a fern,
To share, to help,
To bless and serve,
The human body
With every curve,
Being thankful
And giving praise,
Helps to keep my light ablaze.

CHILDHOOD POEMS.

These poems I wrote growing up.

CAGED IN A ZOO.

I'm caged like a prisoner
I want to get out,
I want to be running around and about,
I'm given the same food,
And I get in a mood,
It's not fair; I'm all caged up.

I want to be free in the jungle
I want to play,
Every day,
Especially when it is hot in May,
I want to be out,
Getting about.

People come and stare at me,
Oh, how I wish to be free,
Everyday
Time by time,
Our cages are there
All in line,
I don't like it here,
I want to get out,
I want to be running around and about.

MY CHRISTMAS

I can't wait till Christmas
It's just one more day
I love Christmas
I always play

I like the snow
Get lots of dough
I sometimes watch the telly
And put Christmas pudding in my belly.

MY DAD

He thinks he's a real cool dude,
He enjoys his food
He's often in a mood,
He's a blazing fire
Red red hot,
He's no money machine
He hasn't got a lot,
He loves to wear his jeans,
And feeds me baked beans,
I have to admit
He is quite small
My dad is not a fool
I love my dad no matter what
Even if he smacked my bot.

MY MUM

My mum makes the sunshine
My mum makes the moon glow
My mum makes the flowers pretty
But that's not all she can show
She can make the storm rough
She can make the sea turn wild
But deep down inside
I know she loves her child
Sometimes we scream and shout
But I love her without a doubt
Sometimes we don't show that we care
But we both know it's always there.

RELAX

Bobtail clouds
A gentle breeze
Blowing to the south east,
The hot bright sun
But no work done Because everyone,
Even the boss is taking a vacation.
I feel lazy
Just picking a daisy,
Don't really want to do work,
Don't really care if oven has burnt the Turk,
Cos' I just want to rest.

NIGHT

The sun has gone to bed
With his cuddly ted
But yet it's not cold Outside in the night,

The moon makes the lake sparkle
Like a diamond ring
He looks very happy
I think I can hear him sing

He's got his friends beside him
The big bear and the plough
I often ask myself
What is he doing now?

Is he watching down on me?
Can he read my mind?
Is he very horrible?
Or is he nice and kind?

It's beautiful out there?
I look up to the stars
It's nice and peaceful
No 'broom broom' of the cars

The stars are trying to say something
What are they trying to say?
They are going soon
Because night is turning to day.

Goodbye stars
Goodbye moon
Hope to see you soon.

SUN POEM

The sun is...
A blinding burning octopus
With a mind of its own.
His legs are stretched out wide
He's up there all alone.

He's shining hard,
He's shining bright
He's fighting with all his might

His legs are stretched
It's head is high
He's glancing down
With a golden eye.

IF I WASN'T WATCHING TV

If I wasn't watching TV, I'd rather...

Dance and dance and dance
Or take a trip to France,
I'd do a parachute from the sky,
Or I'd bake a lovely pie
I'd like to play in a band
Or be a gymnast, but I could break my hand
I'd go skiing or scuba diving
In fact, I don't think the TV is entertaining at all.

CHRISTMAS

Lights, tinsel, Christmas tree
Everyone is happy
Including me
No-one remembers the real reason for this,
They just think of mistletoe and a kiss,
Everyone's making a great big fuss
But no one remembers what Jesus did for us.

HAPPY MOTHER'S
DAY NAN

I would like to say
Someone who is...
Gentle, warm and generous,
Giving, nice and humorous
Loving, perfect and sweet
Pretty and petite
Thoughtful, joyful, wonderful,
Cheerful, helpful, beautiful
Excellent and caring
Pleasant and sharing
Great, splendid and kind
Would be very hard to find,
That's why this poem is for you,
You are the best Nan,
Yes, it's true,
You bring me such pleasure,
You are such a treasure.

BIG, BAD BULLY

I know my teeth are crooked,
I know I can't tell the time,
I know my eyes aren't big and bright
But is that such a crime?
There is this boy called Tommy.
He picks on me every day.
Names, punching and spiteful words,
One day, I'll make him pay.
He knocks my confidence sidewards.
He makes me feel so sad,
He makes fun of what I wear,
I think I'm going mad.
He doesn't like the way I sit,
He doesn't like the way I walk,
He doesn't like the way I stand,
He doesn't like the way I talk,
But he's not perfect either,
He's selfish and unkind
So, one day, I will get him back
And scare him from behind.
If you are cruel
To someone small,

Think for just a moment,
They may be kind, gentle, sweet and nice
If you're nasty - you will pay the price,
Because it's what's in the inside that counts.

HELP US WIN

Grow your own,
Can your own,
Don't sit down
And just moan
Don't let Hitler spoil your day,
Take him down and make him pay,
If we don't win this war
We will be very poor,
Grab your spades and help us dig,
Then go home and feed the pig,
You will have plenty to eat
If you fatten up your meat.

LIFE?

I look in the mirror,
I look at me,
I think about,
What I can see.
Why am I here?
And what do I do?
What is the reason
For me and for you?
Before I was born
Where was I?
Did I live before
Then sadly die?
If so,
Why am I back?
Is there a lesson to learn?
Am I on the right track?
There's so many religions to believe in,
I don't know which one to choose from:
Buddhism, Christianity, Catholic and Sikhs
Hindus, Muslims and Jews,
Has our spirit been on journeys
Long, long ago?
Do past lives exist?
That, we'll never know.

VALENTINE'S DAY CARD FOR MY DAD

I think this is a good occasion
To show how much I care,
No matter if there's no one else
I always will be there,
You're the best dad
I could wish for,
I love you every day
I couldn't love you more,
You cheer me up when I am sad
You teach me right from wrong,
I appreciate it very much
Which is why I'm singing this song,
I hope you had a pleasant day
Valentine's cards or not,
I just want you to know
I love you no matter what.

FESTIVALS

Festivals are good and fun
They bring joy to everyone.
On some occasions we eat a lot,
Some are religious and some are not.
We have a symbol for each festival.
Some are big and some are small,
On Thanksgiving we eat turks,
On Guy Fawkes we see fireworks,
On Good Friday we eat a hot cross bun.
On Christmas we give presents to everyone.

HAPPY BIRTHDAY DAD

Birthdays are a special time
For others to show they care,
Even if they are not close by
Their love is always there,
Years ago a child was born
And brought onto this Earth,
A beautiful child, full of joy,
It's you, it was your birth,
I hope this poem shows,
That you mean a lot to me,
I love you with all my heart.
I hope that you can see,
I hope your birthday brings you joy.
As you deserve it all,
Anytime you need someone,
You only have to call,
You're such a treasure to me
And I would just like to say
This is a wonderful time
Cos' you were born upon this day.

LOVE

the most powerful force in the universe

MY LITTLE GIRL

Cuddling on the sofa
In front of the TV,
Going to the beach
And paddling in the sea,
Painting our toes,
Sand beneath our feet,
Absorbing the sun's rays,
Having nice things to eat,
Making memories with my little girl,
Each and every day,
Like stories, cuddles, drawings and work,
And lots we do play.

ONLY ONE MUM

You woke me up with piggy
On the way to France,
You've helped me clean my home
And also pot my plants,
We had fun at aerobics
You took me to gym,
Although you didn't like it
Sometimes you took me to swim,
We didn't often watch TV
But Music often played in our home,
I still love those songs
Now that I am grown,
You bought me makeup
On my 9th birthday,
"Popsy pie"
You would say
Nature programmes with you and Yann
With my blanket over me,
I also enjoyed very much
All our outings to the sea,
Night drives in the car
Where I drifted off to sleep,
You fed us good food

That wasn't cheap,
Each week I cooked you a cake,
With my Nan I did make,
You taught me to care for plants,
You make sure I'm well fed,
Thanks to you I always take my makeup off
Before bed,
When Christabelle was a baby
You took us out regularly,
You got Yann and I a cat each,
Named Blacky and Teddy,
You're a joy and you're fun
And I'm happy you're my mum,
You're more precious than you know,
And loved very much so,
By friends and family,
And especially by me.

NAN

I love my Nan
She is caring and kind
I love my Nan
She's posh and refined
She's really sweet and very petite
She's cheery and bright
And very polite
I love my Nan ever so much
She has a warm gentle touch
She loves to feed us treats
Like Chocolate, biscuits and sweets
My nan was a dancer
She's also good at art
She loves music
And has a kind heart
I love spending time with my Nan
We paint, play and watch TV
We listen to music
She paints flowers and the sea
My nan is a role model
Generous and funny too
She is so funny
She only wears pink and blue

MY BIG BRO YANN

Thinking of when we were kids
And the things we used to do.
Brings back happy memories
Of being with you,
Like on your motorbike,
You'd pick me up from school,
And the kids in class
Thought that was pretty cool,
You'd let me stay up late
When you looked after me,
You were a softie,
And such a sweetie,
On your bike and trick nuts
You gave me a ride
I jogged to keep up
With your stride,
You said think nice thoughts
When I sleep,
Then my dreams will be sweet,
And when I didn't want dinner,
I'd give it to you to eat,
You kept all my secrets growing up
You didn't tell anyone,

When you made 'Yann's special porridge'
You gave Teddy, the cat, some,
I'm glad I'm your little sis
And I'm glad you're my big bro.
You were such a good sibling
I want you to know.

FAMILY HOLIDAY

Jean Claude and Mickey,
Françoise and Jimmy,
Christabelle and Candy,
François and Jeremy
Enjoyed our holiday
As a family,
We all swam in the sea,
Which was refreshing and lovely,
Even my mum got in,
And cooled down with a swim,
Christabelle and Françoise
Looked for fishes,
And we ate
Such good dishes,
The fruit and veg was tasty,
Ice cream and croissants too,
We visited places
With a lovely view,
We went for long walks,
My mum talks and talks
I would like to communicate more
And speak French fluently,
It's a shame,

It's such a pity,
The adults drank wine,
And the choice was fine,
Aperitif, starter, main course and dessert
And don't forget all the cheese,
The sun was nice and warm
With a pleasant breeze,
Mickey and Jean Claude
Have got holidays done to a tea,
And going on holiday with them
Makes me happy.

DEAR DAD

Now that I've grown up
I would like to say,
You're very special to me
And it'll always be that way,
Thinking back to when I was small
And the things we used to do,
Brings back happy memories
Of being with you,
Teaching me to ride my bike
And teaching me to swim,
Taking me on holidays
And sending me to gym,
Thank you for the things you did
And the things that you still do,
I hope I can be as good
A parent as you.

WHAT I WISH FOR YOU

I wish that every morning
You feel refreshed and alert,
I wish that during your days
You feel happy and no hurt,
I wish that in the evenings
You rest and feel at peace,
I wish you feel content
As you drift off to sleep,
I wish you little luxuries
Each and every day,
I wish you enjoy your life
And be healthy in every way
I wish you love and care
From those around you,
I wish you fun and laughter
And all your dreams come true.

LEANNE

We've been through good times
We've been through bad,
We've shared our joys
You've helped when I've been sad,
You're funny, you're sweet,
You're friendly and petite,
You have your flaws too,
Like all of us do,
But you're my mate
And I love you.

KAY

She's strong and smart
A work of art,
Has fiery red hair
Her dress sense has flair,
She wants to fight
For what is fair.
She reminds me of a battling
Warrior princess,
She's feminine
She can pull off a dress.
She bought me toothless
Who I cuddled at night,
Which made me feel better
She loves to write,
She bought lots of gifts,
On my birthday
I love my dear friend
Beautiful Kay
She's friendly and outgoing
Talks to anyone
She cracks jokes
She's youthful and fun,
She's a warrior in battle

Fighting, going strong,
She's a graceful ballerina
En pointe, expressing her song,
She's thoughtful, loving and kind,
Though she has trouble in her mind,
She's a fierce volcano
Angry with those who do wrong,
For her healing
I do long.

FRIENDS

Migle is a special one,
Together we've had lots of fun,
She's pretty and sensitive
And she has a funny son.

Baby face Kay
Ballerina girl,
Strong and lovely
Give us a twirl,

Paula with a pure heart,
Homely and strong,
She loves tinker bell
And loves to sing a song.

Leanne is cheery
Bubbly and bright,
She looks after herself
She is little in height.

Emma you're a sweet girl,
And precious like a pearl.

Little Linnie bright light,
Soaring to a new height,
Cheeky, bold, full of fun,
Sunny and a funny one.

SIBLING BOND

He taught me to tell the time,
On the P.C how to rhyme,
He looked after me when I was small,
I was short and he was tall,
I would jog
As he walked down the lane,
When I was annoying
He called me Popsy pain,
Tall with long hair,
Looking tough,
Appearances
Are a bluff,
The sweetest softie
I've ever known,
When there was no heating
He didn't moan,
He named his cat Teddy
They were alike,
He gave me a ride,
On his bike,
A sibling bond can be strong,
They make us feel like we belong.

HOME GROUP

There's power where two or three agree,
Thank you all for what you've done for me,
And a special thanks to Anne and Audrey
For all that you've given me,
The laughter, the tears
And singing a song,
Thank you
For helping us all along,
May the love of the father
Grace of the son,
And fellowship of the Holy Spirit
Be with everyone,
We are in Christ
A family,
So let's give a cheer
For Anne and Audrey.

ROSIE

I love my cat Rosie,
She is very small,
She is black and white
She comes running when I call,

She brushes up against me
And purrs at my feet,
She likes cream and cheese,
Which I give her as a treat,

She licks our hands and toes
And puts her head in our shoes,
Out of all the cats in the world
She is the one I would choose.

MY CAT

My cat's the best cat in the world
And she belongs to me,
She purrs when I kiss my lips
She's as happy as can be,
She curls up next to me
And begins to purr,
Even before
I stroke her,
When she was little and went outside
She chased every butterfly and bee,
She was excited over everything
It was beautiful to see,
I talk to her like a baby
She likes it and starts to purr,
I give the best food that I can give
So soft and silky is her fur,
She snuggled in with the teddies
And looked like one too,
My daughter and I laughed and laughed
But she didn't have a clue,
As if to hold my hand
On me she placed her paw,
Sometimes when she's sleeping

We can hear her snore,
I like it when she walks on me
Her little gentle touch,
Oh my cat Rosie
I love her so much.

A FURRY FRIEND

Their companionship is treasure,
Beyond measure,
They'll believe in you
Until you do too,

Loyal and enjoying life
Lesson's humans can learn,
The love you give
Will return,

They never take you for granted
And appreciate all you give,
Food, a bed, a roof over their head,
Treats and a place to live,

When a friend you are in need,
They'll be by your side indeed,
They'll believe the best,
And cuddle you so you can rest,

Thinking of getting a pet,
That you won't neglect,
If you want to love and give,
Give a rescue a chance to live,

An encounter with an animal
Big or small,
Is a joy
And can delight all,

I believe...
Animals belong in the wild
Where they can run and hunt and roam,
But if you're committed to providing
Then share your home,

Showing each other you care,
The times you share,
They'll live in your heart forever,
Now changed for the better,

So if you're looking for a pet to befriend,
And are happy for them to on you depend,
Then I do recommend,
Investing in a furry friend.

VARIETY IS THE SPICE OF LIFE

Here are some poems on various different subjects.

BE YOURSELF

Always be true to yourself,
Don't copy anyone else,
Inspire,
Reinforce what you desire,
Look after your health,

When you lie to others,
To yourself you lie,
'Honesty is the best policy'
This I do buy,

People regret not doing things
More than the things they did,
As you step out of your comfort zone,
Fears, you will rid.

You're unique - cannot be replaced
And only you have what you can give,
Using one's talents
Is a good way to live.

Follow your dreams
Give it all you've got,
For you could gain
Or lose a lot,

It pays to be on your own side,
It helps one enjoy the ride,
Not high and mighty
Nor insignificant and small,
But accepting oneself
Warts and all,

Be yourself
The right people will like you,
Enjoy being you
No one else will do.

OPPORTUNITIES TODAY

What opportunities do you have today
To help someone on their way?
Change the world
One act of kindness at a time,
For we all have a mountain
We are trying to climb,
A text, a hand,
A thoughtful gift,
When we help others
Our own spirits lift,
We all have needs
For others to meet,
Like a jigsaw
We make each other complete,
As I drift off
I think about tomorrow,
How to bless
Or help someone out of their sorrow,
There's opportunities
Every day,
For an act of kindness
Or nice word to say.

RESILIENCE

Rain on your hike,
Having your enemies strike,
Others putting you down,
But not a reason to frown,

With every good dream
There's bumps in the road
Like a river running to the sea,
It keeps at it
Consistently,
Until the vision's a reality,

It's rarely or never
Straightforward,
Look after your needs, do good deeds,
Prevent yourself getting slaughtered,

Exercise, socialise and hobbies too
All play a part in keeping us well,
Keep on learning
And negative thoughts dispel,

Keep your dreams alive,
Feed what gives you drive,
Music, dreaming and belief,
Don't give up if the journey's not brief,

Time out with friends, meals and fun,
Help to get the job done,
Taking in the sights on the way,
Enjoy the whole journey, work, rest and play,

A home, a family of your own,
A business with brilliance,
Older and wiser, with lessons learned,
Such as perspective and resilience.

HIGH ACHIEVEMENT

It's good to get A-C's,
In your GCSE's,
Great is it too,
To pass an interview,

But it's not about snazzy shoes
Or a convertible car,
But more about
How kind you are,

He may have a nice house,
But is he caring to his spouse?
She may have nice hair,
But spread gossip everywhere,

It's wise to be aware,
Of where we can show care,
Of people who may need you there,
It's also good for our welfare,

But adhere,
Your love must be sincere,
And don't neglect those dear,
To those that are near,

Encourage others to reach their best,
Believe that they can pass the test,
And if there's fear still to try,
To soar and fly high in the sky,

Don't let your action
Be a small fraction
Of the love that is really there,
Like an Iceberg in the sea
You can't see completely
Show others that you care,

At a funeral loved ones speak
And share good memories,
They speak of your kindness
And good qualities.

WALKING TO SCHOOL

Feeling the fresh air
And breathing it in,
Makes me happy
And want to sing
I sing about the flowers,
The sky and the trees,
I sing about the blossom.
The birds and the bees,
I chat to my friends along the way,
I chat about
What we will do today.
We stop for a minute
To stroke a cat.
He's all fluffy and soft.
He's cute and fat
So do not drive
Walk instead,
Don't just take
What I said
Try it for yourself
And you will see
Seeing the sun
Makes one happy,

Adoring the gardens
Along the way
Is a great way
To start the day.

AWE AND WONDER

How do those clouds stay in the sky?
The complexity of an eye,
How I can listen to any song,
And how do muscles keep one strong?
My cat can sense when I'm sad
And gives me a hug,
How interesting the life
Of a little bug,
Awe and wonder everywhere
Such as smell and sight,
When I enjoy such things
Life is a delight.

SEIZE THE DAY

Make the most of opportunities
That come your way,
There may not be tomorrow
So seize the day,

Don't put off for tomorrow
What you can do today,
There may not be another chance
So seize the day,

By all means plan ahead,
Make peace before bed,
With loved ones communicate,
In your heart hold no hate,

All the people that you know,
Do what you can to brighten their glow,
All can make a difference I believe,
When you give you too receive,

Don't start tomorrow
Start today,
And do what you can
To seize the day.

BEAUTIFUL BUTTERFLY

I came across a butterfly
With a damaged wing,
Not pitying himself
But happy in the spring,
Enjoying the breeze
Fluttering in the sun,
Sipping nectar
Having fun,
Sweet, delicate
Pretty, a delight,
I thought to myself
What a beautiful sight,
Scars can make one more beautiful
Than what was there before,
Wiser and more compassionate
From the suffering one bore,
In that moment I was inspired
To be a better me,
To allow good to come from bad
And be all that I can be.

GOALS

Reach your goals
One step at a time
And you will find
That mountain you can climb,
Celebrate your achievements
Along the way,
Baby steps
Every day,
Count your blessings
One by one,
You'll find the journey
A lot more fun,
Keep on going
One step at a time,
Sing a song
Or create a rhyme,
Look at your
Next step ahead,
Anticipate good
Do not dread,
Believe in yourself
Give it a try,
Be creative

Don't be shy,
Be humble,
Not proud,
A silver lining
Has every cloud,
Don't give up, don't give up
Find another way,
Isn't this what Churchill
And Einstein did say,
Eat, sleep and rest
Is what others say,
Keep focused
Do not stray,
Work hard, play and rest,
Acknowledge all of your progress,
Expect a breakthrough,
Have faith in all you do.

A RAINBOW OF COLOURS

I know that you know,
It takes different colours to make a rainbow,
Likewise it takes different people
To make the world go round,
Some to dream big,
Some with their feet on the ground,
Inventors, through electricity
Brought us light,
Children,
Who bring delight,
Cooks to feed,
Librarians to read,
Parents to provide
A child's need,
Nurses to nurse,
Cleaners to clean,
Youth workers to guide
A troublesome teen,
Police,
To keep society in line,
To protect,

And fight crime,
Dancers to inspire,
Teachers to teach,
Volunteers
Who clean up the beach,
Embrace your true colours
For they make you who you are,
Shine bright
Be a star.

EVERY LITTLE DOES COUNT

Each smile to a stranger
Each kind word to a friend,
Each card
That one does send,
Each prayer said,
Each tummy fed,
Each thoughtful gift,
Every lift,
Disciplining a child,
To show the right way,
Having fun also,
Making time to play,
We can all make a difference,
Every little does count,
Let's do what we can,
So it's be a big amount.

WOMEN ARE WONDERFUL

Delicate features
A sweet nose,
Elegant hands
And dainty toes,
Good at communicating
Has fun dressing up,
Sweet,
A precious pup,
Being a good homemaker,
Making a house a home,
Keeping things clean,
With polish and foam,
Not doing all the cleaning as such,
But giving the house a feminine touch,
Working hard,
Her family are blessed
Looks after her household,
Bringing out the best,
The perfect companion
For a man,
Supporting him

Where she can,
Sensitive
To others needs,
Caring
And always feeds,
A precious Pearl
Worth more than gold,
Fragile and pretty
Perfect to hold.

SNOW

I love to walk in the snow
When it's fresh and brand new,
Feeling it crunch beneath my feet
To run and kick in it too,
Every snowflake is unique
Can this really be true,
When I think of all the snow
And in Antarctica too,
The patterns you can see
When it lands in one's hair,
A snow day is an opportunity
To play without care,
To slide and sledge
And ski down a hill,
Is fun
At my age still,
When the sun shines
Clear and bright,
I see glittery sparkles
Silver and white,
Winter to an African
A sugar dusted land?
Cold but beautiful

With snow instead of sand,
Each country beautiful
In its own way,
African sunsets
English gardens, with clouds of grey,
We can't drive, we can't work,
So let's go out and play
Snowmen, igloo, there's lots to do,
Let's just have a wonderful day.

WILDLIFE

A fish is designed
To swim all day long,
A bird is designed
To sing a song,
A bunny alert
To danger around,
A hunting cat,
Makes virtually no sound,
Man's best friend
Is a dog,
A crocodile is disguised
As a log,
Ants so small,
Giraffes so tall,
Whales so big,
Moles constantly dig,
Plants bring peace,
And positivity increase,
Tiny creatures
That live in the lawn,
How precious to see
A lamb being born,
A cheetah has speed,

A tree comes from a seed,
Water keeps on flowing,
Plants keep on growing,
In nature I recharge
So much to see,
More interesting
Than watching TV,
I love spending time outdoors
No matter the time of year,
When I'm in nature
My mind is clear.

A DIAMOND IN THE ROUGH

Instead of laughing
Lending a hand,
Standing up for good
Making a stand,
Expressing yourself
Being true to who you are,
Makes one
Shine like a star,
But people will try
To treat you like dirt,
Stab you in the back
And say words that hurt,
Pressures at home
And also at work,
Worries and wrong thinking
Around tempting they lurk,
Physical and
Emotional pain
Like gold being purified
Again and again,
Learning limits

And what puts one in pain,
So not to be refined
Again and again,
Tired and hungry
With a million things to do,
Seeking
What is true,
A wise woman said
"Ask what can I learn?"
So ones thinking
Starts to turn,
I'll grow better not bitter
From all that hurt,
Like a diamond is formed
In the dirt.

TRUE BEAUTY

Being the shape you're meant to be,
Making the most of that,
Healthy and wise,
Not telling lies,
Not focused on being too fat,

Recognising weaknesses
And doing your best,
Working hard
Taking time to rest,

Appreciating you,
To yourself being true,
A positive mind
Being loving and kind,

A genuine smile,
Is so worthwhile,
Loving the skin,
That you are in,

Being willing
To learn and grow,
Knowing all of it
You do not know,

The world says you're beautiful
If you fit this mould,
But true beauty is having
A heart of gold,

Love is what's beautiful
Through and through,
Embrace yourself
Enjoy being you.

PRECIOUS YOU

When you feel lonely
Remember Jesus did too,
He was abandoned at the cross
So he could relate to you,

When you feel scared
Remember Jesus did too,
He sweat blood
So he could relate to you,

When you feel pain
Remember Jesus did too,
His flesh was pierced with nails
So he could relate to you,

All that Jesus
Did go through,
Was for
Precious you.

SIMPLE PLEASURES, PRICELESS TREASURES

Waking up
Early and bright,
Having your hearing
Having your sight,
Enjoying small talk
That perks one up,
Stopping to stroke
A joyful pup,
Enjoying nature
Feeling the breeze,
Our problems
They do ease,
Sending messages
Showing you care,
Joy is doubled
When you share,
Reading
And writing,
What you find
Exciting,

This is what
I have found,
That simple pleasures
Are all around.

LIFE IS PRECIOUS

To see my loved ones' faces
And their radiant smile,
Makes my journey
More worthwhile,

To taste clean water
And feel a warm shower,
Cotton on the skin
And the beauty of a flower,

Weights in the gym
Fresh air as you run,
A bubbly drink
With warmth of the sun,

Life is precious
In many ways,
So let's make the most
Of all of our days,

Watching the birds build a nest,
Keeping the sabbath a day of rest,
To see, to smell, to taste, to touch,
So much to experience, oh, so much,

Baby's cheeks,
Teach what you know,
So they can learn,
Flourish and grow,

Sand between your toes,
Grass beneath your feet,
Enjoying simple pleasures
Makes life sweet,

Stories, art, playing with kids,
Sleeping, when feeling heavy are your lids,
Waking refreshed when it's early still,
Having the afternoon to chill,

Acts of kindness to show you care,
Someone playing with your hair,
Putting your feet up in an arm chair,
There is beauty everywhere.

SUNDAY

Time to rest
Time to play,
Time to restore
So I feel okay,
Everybody
Needs to rest,
Take time out
To feel their best,
Sit back and enjoy
The work that's been done,
And give praise to Father, spirit,
And son.

FABULOUS FOOD

Lemon in the morning
Herb tea at night,
Eating healthily
Is such a delight,
Making me alert
Is the sharpness of lime,
It's good to eat
At a regular time,
Food is precious
Every bite,
Not feeling heavy,
But nice and light,
The occasional treat
Whatever that may be,
Apple crumble,
Or scone with cream tea,
Salad with hummus
Or veggies, rice and meat,
Free range and organic is best,
And for dessert something sweet.

REPETITION
REINFORCES

The branches of a tree
Look like the brain,
The thicker branches
Are thoughts engrained,
Repeating thoughts
Strengthen the route,
It's time to change
If it's not bearing good fruit,
Challenge values
And ideas,
Overcoming
Irrational fears,
Ask
"Is there a lesson that I can learn"
So that things
Begin to turn,
Sleep and stimulation
Play a part,
In looking after
This work of art,
God's word shines a light

And exposes wrong thinking
So that our thinking
Is not stinking,
Being aware of one's thoughts
Is a bright idea,
Protect your brain
For it is dear,
Our mind is powerful,
An effective tool,
More precious
Than any jewel.

WHAT IS YOUR WHY?

What is the reason
You do what you do,
For your why is the reason
You follow it through,
Why are you up in the morning?
Why are you here on earth?
What is your calling?
Why did your mum give birth?
It may be big
It may be small,
It may not be
What you learned in school,
What is your passion?
What is your dream?
What makes you happy?
What makes you beam?
Simple actions can mean a lot
And go a long long way,
Kindness is a chain reaction
And could make someone's day,
How do you want to make a difference?
Dig down deep,
What you sow

You will reap,
Compassion and care
Goes a long way,
You shape the future
With what you do today.

NATURE

Penguins propose with a pebble
Bees die to defend their nest,
Clear diamonds form
When earth is compressed,

The heart of a shrimp
Is located in its head,
A growing snake
Does its old skin shed,

In different directions
Do chameleons move their eyes,
Eagles use
Hot air to rise,

When travelling
Sea horses link tails,
The largest creatures on earth
Are whales,

All clownfish Are born male,
Sleep for three years Does a snail,

When puppies play
They let girls win,
A stick insect
Is incredibly thin,

An odour
Is the weapon of a skunk,
Baby elephants
Suck their trunk,

Give us oxygen
Do trees,
In winter
Wood frogs freeze,

Otters have the thickest fur,
No one knows how cats purr,
Crows play pranks on one another,
Birds kiss their significant other,

Butterflies taste with their feet,
Prairie dogs kiss to greet,
Dragon flies form a heart shape,
When they mate,

Bats catch prey in pitch black,
The bonds of a wolf pack,
Cows can have a best friend,
Some jelly fish lives never end.

CARE FOR ALL,
GREAT AND SMALL

Let's be an inspiration,
Let's be a caring nation,
Let's fight,
For what is right,
Let's see,
Animals go free,
Let animals live
Where they belong,
Where they can dance
And sing their song,
A ray of daffodils
Is a beautiful sight,
And so is standing up
For what is right,
It's pleasant to see
Animals in the wild,
It brings delight
To an adult or child,
Let the fish
Swim in the sea,
Where they are
Supposed to be,

Prepare the animals
To live outside
Of captivity,
To see animals
Bored in the zoo,
Makes me
Extremely blue,
It's the right
Thing to do,
To put an end
To the zoo.

FRIENDSHIPS

Good times are not as much fun,
Bad times weigh a ton,
When there's no one with you to share,
To lend a hand or care,
When others give an ear,
And take time to hear,
What you're going through,
Doesn't seem so blue,
In times of distress and despair,
The company of those who care,
Build you up and make you strong,
And help you to get along,
You can help each other see
In a different light,
Where things look
A prettier sight,
You can help each other
Learn and grow,
As life tosses you
To and fro.

STORMS

I have written these poems in difficult times, but they finish on a positive note.

DEAR GOD

The stresses and strain
Is driving me insane,
I need your soothing peace
I need the pressures to cease,
God, I know you can hear me
And so, I pray,
That you will soothe me
And things will be ok,
I pray God I'll be happy
And enjoy my life,
I pray for an end
To the struggles and strife,
God, I pray for peace
And a healthy mind too,
I pray that we'll be close
And I will please you,
I pray I pray I pray
That you'll help me find my way,
I need your guidance
I need your light,
I need my future
To be bright.

MEDICATED ZOMBIE

I want to wake with a spark
And have a twinkle in my eye,
I want to have good posture
And hold my head up high,
I want to work hard
And reach my best,
I want to be positive
And not be distressed,
I want to be healthy
So, I feel great,
I want to enjoy my life
And what I've got to appreciate,
I want to come off medicine
And be who I'm supposed to be
I don't want to be
A drowsy zombie,
I want to have peace with God
And myself,
I want to bless my family
And for us to have good health.

A NEW SONG

I want to be yours
Forever and ever,
And praise you in life
No matter the weather,
Because I know
I belong to you
Thank you for the beauty of
The morning dew,
And all the other lovely times
I've shared and had,
And thank you for
My daughter and dad,
Who have helped me,
And do what they can,
Please bless them Lord
And Nan and Yann,
And don't forget
My mum and Lee,
Who have also
Helped me,
Because you're wonderful
And you're great,
You can make

Our paths straight,
You heal the broken hearted,
You comfort those in need,
You bring joy and peace
You guide and lead,
You mend a broken life
You bring peace of mind,
You bring real hope
You are caring and kind,
You are beautiful and amazing
You are powerful and strong,
You do miracles
You forgive our wrong,
Now I'm your child
To you I belong,
You transform us
And give us a new song.

GOD'S BLESSINGS

The pleasure of food
And nourishment it brings,
When our heart is glad
And out it sings,
My daughter playing
With my hair,
When people show
That they care,
Playing with my daughter
Having lots of fun,
I'm glad I can be
A silly mum,
Walking through the country
The rustling leaves,
Seeing pretty sights
The gentle breeze,
Receiving a smile
Getting together with your mates,
Meeting new people
And making dates,
Trying new looks,
Reading interesting books,

Trees and plants,
To run and dance,
I cannot write them all down,
So be cheery and do not frown.

MY CUP OVERFLOWS

These poems are expressing gratitude and joy after experiencing God being at work in my life.

GRATITUDE

I'm grateful for
The summer breeze,
I'm grateful for
The peaceful trees,
I'm grateful for the dewy grass,
I'm grateful for the beautiful sky,
I'm grateful Jesus is with me
And he reigns from on high,
I'm grateful God has opened my eyes
To the beauty all around,
I'm grateful he offers his people
A mind that is sound,
I'm grateful to God
Coz he made me glad,
I'm grateful to God
He helps when I'm sad,
I'm grateful to God
For all of his love,
I'm grateful to God
Coz he sees from above,
I'm grateful for his care,
And because he's always there,
How wonderful God's wisdom

How wonderful God's grace,
How wonderful God's mercy
How wonderful God's embrace,
I'm grateful God has healed me
In so many ways,
I'm grateful God is with me
All of my days,
I'm grateful for my family
I'm grateful for my friends,
My thankfulness to God
Just never ever ends.

WONDER

My washing smells nice
My house is clean,
The many blessings
That are often unseen,
I thank him for fresh air
I thank him I am well,
The wonders he's done
I have to tell,
My autumn and winter
Was not dark this year,
It was not filled
With anxiety or fear,
Who would of thought
I'd be in this place now,
To the one almighty
I do bow,
I have hope and faith
My days with God'll be good,
He healed me
Like I knew he could,
Dreams I had
Are coming true,
I'm so grateful to God
For pulling me through.

MY THANKS TO GOD

My thanks to God
I want to give,
For my house
And where I live,
For the people
In my life,
For getting me through
Struggles and strife,
For healing me
Deep within,
Not throwing me
In the bin,
For guiding me
Throughout my days,
For helping me
In all my ways,
For his patience
And his love,
For all his gifts
From above,
Because he's lovely
Because he's kind,
Because he's forgiving

And puts the past behind,
I want to show I'm thankful
For Gods mercy and grace,
I want to express my love
And for us to embrace,
He's blessed me with peace
And with joy my heart now sings,
He's helped me appreciate
Simple little things,
Like trees and flowers,
Animals and showers,
Food and drink and snow,
He guides me everyday
In the way I should go.

PRAISE GOD

Praise God
He's magnificent,
And I want to say
I love God
In every way,
I love God almighty
He's the only one,
He's the only one
Who can forgive through the son,
God is my friend
And also, my Lord,
Out onto me
His love and grace he's poured,
I love God and I want to serve
I want to make him pleased and glad,
I want to show his love and compassion
And help those which are sad,
I'm grateful for my blood family
My friends and spiritual family too,
I'm grateful because God
I belong to you,
God's been good to me,
I love my family,

I love my friends as well,
The good news I want to tell,
Praise God for his love
Praise God for his care,
Praise God because
He is everywhere,
I love God
Oh yes, I do
He takes care of me
And he can take care of you,
God is magnificent
And he is king,
This my heart
Wants to joyfully sing,
Praise God for the people in my life
Every single one,
And the best companion of all
Jesus the son,
I'm grateful you understand me
Jesus, the son,
I'm glad you understand
Every single one,
You're more wonderful

Than I ever thought,
You helped me
When I've been distraught,
Praise God for the trees
Praise God for the sun,
Praise God because
He loves everyone,
Praise Jesus because
He came to understand man,
And reconcile us to God
He can,
Praise be to the Father
Because he sent his son,
To take away our sins
And he's for everyone,
Praise God for the blessings
He's poured out on me,
Praise God for my friends
And family,
Praise God for the church
That I am in,
Praise God because
He cleanses from sin,

Praise God for my body
It's lasted me well,
The good works of the Lord
I have to tell,
Thank you God
You can move any mountain,
Thank you God
You can cleanse us from sin,
The joy of knowing him
Outweighs anything,
He is God almighty
Sovereign king.

THE BEST

Praise you God
Almighty one,
For joy, laughter
Friends and fun,
Because you are wise
And know what is best,
Because you offer
Peace and rest,
Because our sorrow
You do know,
Because compassion
You do show,
Because your love
Goes on and on,
I want to sing
A happy song,
For flowers, creatures
Sun and fresh air,
Because you are
Everywhere,
Because you are king
Of everything,
Because you are

Just and fair,
Because I know
You are right,
Because you make
Our load light,
Praise for your joy
Praise for your peace
Praise for your love
That will not cease,
Thank you
For all of my friends,
And your love
That never ends,
Thank you God
For genuine rest,
God you are
The very best.

HOW WONDERFUL

How wonderful it is
To enjoy the fresh air,
How wonderful it is
That God is everywhere,
How wonderful it is
That the birds cheerfully sing,
How wonderful it is
That Christ is king,
How wonderful it is
To have a nice home,
How wonderful it is
That God is on the throne,
How wonderful it is
That God is in my heart,
How wonderful it is
That he can give a fresh start,
How wonderful it is
That he loves to hear us sing,
How wonderful it is
To God, glory we can bring.

GOD'S GRACE IS
IN THIS PLACE

He didn't have to wake
Me today,
Or journey with me
Along the way,
He didn't have to give me
Food to eat,
Or tasty treats
That are sweet,
He didn't have to bless me
With good friends and family,
He didn't have to die
So, I could be free,
He looks at who we are
And doesn't bring up old sin,
He sees the best in us
A reflection of him.

THE CHURCH

A place to make friends
A place to learn and grow,
A place to get strengthened
So, your light can show,
Doing what you can
To serve the community,
Being your best
And having a cup of tea,
God loves
To celebrate,
I never knew church
Would be this great,
Lots of fun for everyone,
Youth, young and old,
Finding safety
In the fold,
God created us all
And can relate to everyone,
He knows at times we fail
Which is why he sent his son.

YOU PROVIDE

When I was hungry
You provided food,
You've provided
So I could change my mood,
When I was homeless
You provided a house,
At the right time
You provided a spouse,
When I was lonely
You did send,
The right people
To be a friend,
When I was bored
You provided clubs,
When I was desperate
You provided hugs,
Once I'd tried two
You provided a church,
Where to know you
I began my search,
At times being poor
You've provided cash,
You provide dock leaves

For a nettle rash,
You provide each day
For us to work, rest and play,
You bless abundantly
When we obey.

THANK YOU

Thank you that you do provide,
And you are by my side,
I am wonderfully and fearfully made,
You have answered when I've prayed,
I have hands to hold
And feet to walk,
A body to dance
And a mouth to talk,
Talk of how good you've been,
And of all the miracles that I've seen.

MY CUP OVERFLOWS

Praise God for the flowers
Praise God for the trees,
Praise God for the birds,
And for the bees,
God is my friend
My saviour, my all,
God is awesome
And he does rule.

SHORT AND SWEET

Sometimes written
At the end of the day
To help me
On my way.

Just a few words to
express what I want to say.

I'm alive I'm alive
Hip hip hooray,
So, I'm going to make
The most of my day.

Praise you God
You gave me the best of care,
Praise you God
You see everywhere.

Thank you, you helped me give up smoking
And blessed me when I did,
Thank you Jesus
That our sin you rid.

The fresh clean air
So clear and pure and cool,
I'm so Glad that God is king
And he does rule,
Going for a walk
In the morning sun,
Breathing the air
And going for a run,
This is definitely
A great way
To start
A fabulous day.

Praise God almighty
Almighty God almighty!

Thank you, dear God for this new day,
Thank you, you are the potter, and we are the clay,
You mould us and make us into what we should be,
Like a beautiful strong blossoming tree.

God you are real and strong
And funny too,
God you are lovely
There is none like you.

I love to wake up early
After a good night's sleep,
But still joy comes in the morning
Even after a night of weep,
When you have a cold night
God can be so close,
Speaking comforting words
Things you need to know.

Father o Father
You're such a delight,
Lord Jesus
You're whiter than white,
Holy Spirit
You help us fight the good fight,
Together you shine
Ever so bright.

Dear Father God
Thank you for soft socks
Thank you for cotton clothes,
Thank you, you help us to be
Like a blossoming tree that grows.

Praise you for fresh air
Clean water and cool breeze,
Thank you you help us to blossom
Like strong beautiful trees.

Celebrate achievements
Even if they're small,
And regularly
Achievements, recall.

I don't think there is greater joy
Than to worship you,
I am touched when you express
How much you love me too.

Thank you that today
I got the needed rest
Thank you I no longer feel
Pain or pressure upon my chest.

I'm delighted to spend
My life with you,
And an
Eternity too.

Thank you so much for all you do
And for what you've done,
You love us so much
That you gave us your son.

To wake each morning
Knowing you're around,
Makes my heart joyful
Keeps my mind sound,
I walk with you
Talk with you
Share with you each day,
My hopes, dreams

Thoughts and faults
Along the way,
I love us to dance
It's so much fun,
God, you're the great "I Am"
There is only one.

I cannot give you enough praise
I need others to join in,
For what you went through
To wash away our sin.

God, I want to give you all that I can
Because you deserve so much,
You dance with me when I'm happy
And you comfort me with your touch.

Thank you dear God
We all have gifts to use
Thank you too
You took away my winter blues.

Seek his heart
Not his hand.

God no one can describe you
Although we try,
The cross says it all
For us you did die.

Don't let your to do list
Dictate to you,
But dictate
To your list of things to do.

It's good to have
A cheerful heart,
So, counting your blessings
Is a good start.

Right people
Right time,
God you are
So divine.

You've done so many miracles
I'm amazed,
I'm flabbergasted
I look up and gaze.

I needed a certain scripture
From the big book,
So, I picked it up
And took a random look,
Heaven's galore
It was highlighted right there,
Just one of the ways
You showed you care.

Be thoughtful
And show love,
This will please
Heaven above.

Doing just a few
Things each day
Does go
A long way.

Little things
Mean a lot,
Like a drink
When it's hot.

Early to bed
Rested head.

Only you could take the bad
And turn it to lessons we use,
So, we become better
And what's better we choose.

Thank you for the gift of every day,
I want to live them your way.

I was so tired, exhausted and weak,
Often I did weep,
I read "you'll take afternoon naps without a worry
You'll enjoy a good night's sleep"
I thought naps would be taking the Micky,
I can't afford to be that picky,
But to sleep well at night,

Without a fight,
Would do me alright,
So, to sleep well at night I did pray,
Now not only do I sleep well at night,
But I also have naps in the day!

Sing praises sing praises
To the king,
For he is ruler of everything,
Sing praises sing praises
To the lord,
For he gives us armour
And his word as a sword,
Sing praises sing praises
For it is good,
To sing glad songs
Like we should.

A rhyme a day
Helps me on my way.

Speak up for what is right,
For justice fight.

God has a plan and purpose for my pain.

On the other foot
Put the shoe,
So, you'll know
What to do.

Start today
Right away.

Think for too long,
And the opportunities gone.

Instead of trying
To always improve,
Enjoy yourself
And you will move.

Listen to music and chill,
So good I will feel.

Eat breakfast to feel strong,
All day long.

Enjoy the process,
Appreciate the progress.

Make the most of the day,
And opportunities that come your way.

Enjoy the work you do,
And celebrate too.

Be aware,
God is there.

If you feel it's wrong,
Don't carry on.

Praise through the progress.

TO FINISH

Here are a few
poems to finish.

ALIVE AND WELL

It is good
To be alive and well,
To share the story
I have to tell,
I was distraught
Now I have a life to live,
My thanks and praise
I want to give,
To wake in the morning
Bright and strong,
And to sing
A happy song,
Always someone worse off
Enjoy what you've got,
Whether that's a little
Or a lot,
Every day
There're simple pleasures,
Special moments
That are treasures,
Living life to the full

For our last we don't know,
Giving thanks and praise
Through my days
Makes my cup overflow.

YOU'RE INDESCRIBABLE

Bees defend to the death
With a sting,
A defence mechanism
Has every living thing,
Flowers
With each fragrance unique,
Uplifting when
Things look bleak,
The bonds of a wolf pack
And loyalty of a dog
Are extraordinary
And how a tadpole turns to a frog,
Elephants know
Huge areas of land,
And how nice it is
To hold a hand,
Pink and white blossom
Show your gentle care,
Plants are significant
They give us clean air,
You're strong like a lion
Gentle like a lamb,
I try to describe you
But nobody can.

IT IS GOOD TO BE ALIVE

Watching the sunrise
Sipping a drink,
To sit quietly
Being able to think,
Listening to music
Tapping one's feet,
At the end of a meal
Having something sweet,
Saunas
And cold showers,
Blossom
And flowers,
The breeze
Through one's hair,
Cake
To share,
Walking bare feet,
Hearing the birds' tweet,
Going to sleep,
Waking up,
Playing
With a precious pup,
Lifting weights

Enjoying a jog,
Going for a walk,
Patting a dog,
It is good
To be alive,
To learn and grow
Flourish and thrive.

Lightning Source UK Ltd.
Milton Keynes UK
UKHW010335050921
389926UK00001B/92

9 781665 585040